MW01291637

The Holistic Self-Assessment

By Derrick Broze

The Holistic Self Assessment
Written By Derrick Broze
Edited by Carey Wedler
Cover Design by AH Solomon

Contents 2

Each chapter is designed to help the reader answer a specific question that can assist them in their assessment. The questions are as follows:

1. Who am I?
2. What are my principles?
3. What are my goals?
4. What are my habits? Are they aligned with my principles and goals? Where are my words inconsistent with my actions?
5. How can I think holistically about my goals?
6. Are my relationships in line with my principles and goals?
7. What are the roots of my inconsistencies and my fears?
8. What exercises/practices/rituals will help me release these fears and inconsistencies?
9. What steps will I take to integrate these exercises and this knowledge?
10. How can I share my takeaways from this assessment with others and hold myself accountable?

Acknowledgements:

Thank you to every single person who seeks healing and growth. Thank you to all those who have shared valuable lessons with me. No matter how the lessons came – through pain or through joy – I give thanks for every opportunity for growth. I share gratitude and appreciation with every person who inspires me to continue working to be the best version of myself.

Foreword

Have you ever struggled with discovering your purpose in life? Have you ever wondered where you are going? Have you asked tough questions like *"Who am I"*? Have you tried to augment your life with clear-cut goals, principles, tasks, and guidelines in order to make life's voyage a journey of healing, love, compassion, and kindness? If not, this humble yet impactful volume, written by my friend and colleague Derrick Broze, will provide you with ample instruction and insight to allow you to achieve your full potential as a conscious human being. It may even help you reach what psychologists have called your self-actualized potential, allowing you to live a more enriched and purposeful life.

I realize some people may shy away from books that seem to stink of "guru's knowledge" or amount to nothing more than cleverly concealed snake oil. However, I have had the luxury and pleasure of spending personal time with Derrick. He is an authentic and beautiful soul with plenty of worldly knowledge and experience to share. He has lived a challenging life, which has included spending time locked in a jailhouse for possession of crystal methamphetamine. I have also undergone a similar ordeal, having been arrested for possessing MDMA and cocaine. This is important because I can empathize with Derrick's need to reach out to people and connect with them for the purpose of helping them to heal. Indeed, myriad important life lessons are gleaned from these types of experiences.

I am not saying this grants Derrick some profound or esoteric knowledge that none of us possess, but his background and experiences definitely harbor fertile ground for the growth of wisdom. In this sense, Derrick's prescription for self-healing within *The Holistic Self-Assessment* might be something we all need to pay attention to if we are attempting to better ourselves and the world. After I read the book for the first time, I was shocked by its clarity, usability, and succinct nature. I even had a couple of epiphanies about my own life prior to even conducting the actual self-assessment.

The resources and information Derrick provides on self-healing are also top-notch. He draws from well-known psychologists, such as Abraham Maslow, and prominent figures in the communication space, such as Marshall Rosenberg. Derrick has taken great care to make sure his book contains all the current facts interspersed with the right amount of guidance. I believe this book can help anyone learn to look at themselves more objectively and consider where they want to be in life from a holistic perspective. I don't think anything quite this personal and intimate has been done in the same way before, especially from such a non-judgmental perspective.

I particularly enjoyed the chapter about "Getting to the Root." In this section, Derrick adroitly tackles the issue of childrearing and the crux of our traumas and problems of living. He channels attachment theory and mentions how early traumas can cause problems in life that may damage our ability to live holistically. Derrick then asks us to contemplate our pasts in order to discover some truth. These insights can catalyze our ability to heal and continue building strong bonds with the people we have chosen to spend our lives with. Powerful stuff.

The Holistic Self-Assessment" is the perfect practical use case of Derrick's holistic philosophy, as well as a legitimate workbook for activists who are striving to make the world a better place. I especially recommend it for activists because they don't always seem to be functioning from a place of true happiness and centeredness. After reading through this workbook and following its instruction to examine the self, any activist or wayward soul will be able to come to terms with who they are and build the courage necessary to help heal the whole world.

I know I will be using it often.

-Sterlin Lujan

Introduction

Thank you for choosing to take this journey toward self-healing. I appreciate every person who finds this work and considers employing the practices contained within it. The goal of The Holistic Self-Assessment is to serve as a guide that allows individuals to examine their own lives and identify inconsistencies between their thoughts, words, and actions.

The term holistic is related to the theory known as Holism. Holism is a philosophy concerned with wholes or with complete systems. When examining whole systems rather than the individual pieces of a particular problem, you are likely to come away with a completely different perspective, and thus, a different solution than you would likely find when studying the individual components. We will explore this concept later in the book.

For now, let's just say this particular self-assessment is not about simply changing your diet to organic or adding yoga or meditation to your routine. While I absolutely recommend doing those things, I also believe the answer lies in taking the holistic approach by looking at your entire life and seeking to understand how you relate to the world. What is the relationship between your actions and your family, the political class, the environment, and the culture you live in? Are these relationships and actions aligned with your principles and goals? That is what we aim to find out.

In my experience, I have found that many well-meaning individuals consistently struggle with achieving their goals or living up to what they view as their highest potential. I believe this is because the human species is in need of deep emotional healing. Humanity's history is filled with violence, war, enslavement, rampant environmental destruction, and more recently, the re-emergence of the threat of nuclear war. Not to mention, there are individuals who seek to use the instruments of government and corporate power to enrich themselves.

This has led to the creation of a species whose members exist in various states of recovery from the trauma of the human condition. It is an often overwhelming reality, but it does us no good to deny or ignore it. We can work to change this reality by changing ourselves. Many people also deal with personal trauma from environmental factors experienced throughout childhood. In this state of trauma, it is unsurprising that we are easily manipulated and controlled by external forces, and it is important that we work to reclaim our hearts and minds.

This trauma leads some down the path of self-medication through drugs, inflicting self-harm, and other destructive behaviors. I personally know full well the results of succumbing to unhealthy habits. In November 2005, I was arrested for possession of a controlled substance after being caught with crystal methamphetamine. I was one week away from turning 21 and had been sober off meth for one month after spending the previous ten months racing to rock bottom. Long story short, I had been using various drugs off and on for about 3 years in an effort to

11

escapc my depression and self-esteem issues. I spent most of my youth abusing my body with drugs and inflicting self-harm through cutting, as well as destroying relationships with people I loved.

It took me getting locked up for 18 months to figure out that I wanted to live a different life. I discovered meditation while incarcerated and began to understand the power of self-reflection and healing. I journaled every day for six months and found I was starting to understand the root of my pain and the choices I made while lost on my emotional rollercoaster. The book you are reading is a representation of the steps I took myself through during that period. It is a representation of the process I continue to explore as I work to become the best version of myself that I can be.

One of the major reasons we struggle with our self-worth is that we often set goals that seem appealing enough, but upon closer examination, come to realize they do not actually represent our deepest desires. We are influenced by our parents, friends, the media, and a myriad of other external forces. It can be difficult to recognize whether your life choices and personal habits are a result of your own choosing or one of these external sources.

Either way, this problem illustrates the need for maintaining an open and positive relationship and conversation with ourselves. By developing this dialogue, we can identify our own doubts, fears, and insecurities and work to understand and overcome them. Through this process, I believe we can each work towards actualizing what we see as the highest version of ourselves.

This book is designed to help you in the process of self-actualization, a term that has various meanings in the field of psychology. Abraham Maslow's hierarchy of needs theory asserted that once an individual's basic needs are met, the person can reach their full potential via self-actualization. I define self-actualization as the process of aligning one's external image — the image we portray to others (especially via social media) — and the internal image of ourselves we see in our own mind.

I do not know if human beings are capable of ever actually achieving self-actualization and existing as "perfectly aligned" individuals, but then again, the entire premise is based on subjective standards. Each of us has a different vision of what an ideal life looks like. We each have a different version of "perfection" or happiness. We can benefit from working towards developing as deep a connection to our own hearts and minds as possible. That is where our journey will begin.

Each chapter is designed to answer a question. The answer to these questions will arise through your participation in the readings and exercises. As you answer the questions, you will hopefully start to understand more about how you view yourself and why you make the choices you do. You will also uncover opportunities to make improved choices that are more in line with your values and your goals.

The first chapter starts out with a simple question that is often difficult to answer: Who am I? After getting to know more about your personal view of yourself, you will ask what it means to have principles and what principles currently guide you individually and as human beings. Next, you will look at your goals and habits and ask what it means to live holistically. You will then be given an opportunity to examine all of your current relationships to see if they are in line with your previously stated principles and goals. From there, you will look at the root causes of your inconsistencies and ask what keeps you from achieving your unique goals. Finally, the guidebook offers several exercises to assist you in implementing beneficial changes that will help you live out your vision of your best self. You will also have an opportunity to develop an action plan for moving forward and keeping track of your progress.

This process asks you to open up your heart and mind, set aside any self-doubt or anxiety — or at least be compassionately conscious of it — and consider participating in the assessment one step closer to aligning your internal vision of yourself with the self you present to the world. This guidebook only functions if the reader is an active participant. You will only get back what you put in, so if you choose to hold back some of your deep truths and not be completely honest with yourself, do not expect to experience healing in those areas.

Also, do not expect the unhealthy behaviors that can likely be traced back to these unexplored emotional spheres to magically go away. It took me three trips to state prisons before I finally made the necessary life changes for my next stage of growth. I understood the changes before that point, and I could recite the solutions without hesitation, but it took a bit longer before I was ready to be completely honest with myself and begin the process of healing.

When you answer the questions, take your time. Take in each word, reflect on the meaning, and spend a few minutes meditating on the answer. The more specific and detailed your answers, the deeper your understanding will be.

Remember: This book is meant for you. It is your choice whether you share your findings with anyone, but I believe it will be more beneficial if you are honest and vulnerable when working through the steps. This guidebook is here whenever you need it and as many times as you need it. If the first time you work through it you are not ready to be completely vulnerable, give yourself some time to reflect and come back when you feel more open.

Thank you so much for embarking on this journey towards healing, empowerment, and self-actualization. Together we are contributing towards the emotional, psychological, and spiritual evolution of our species.

Becoming Self Aware

Question: Who am I?

Take a moment to reflect on these three words: *who, am,* and *I*. The word "who" in this sense is an interrogative word, meaning it's designed to answer a question. The word "am" is the present tense first person version of "be" and implies that an object has an objective existence ("I think, therefore I am"). Finally, "I" can be used as a pronoun to describe an individual. In this sense, "I" is defined as "the person who is speaking or writing." Taken together as a question, these words compel us to understand who and what we are interested in being and doing while on this planet. To come to an honest understanding of ourselves and what we are capable of, we ought to examine our personal view of ourselves. First, we should briefly look at the concept of the self.

The dictionary definition of "self" is "the entire person of an individual" or "an individual's typical character or behavior." It is also defined as "the union of elements (such as body, emotions, thoughts, and sensations) that constitute the individuality and identity of a person."

Carl Rogers, an American psychologist and one of the founders of the humanistic school of psychology, believed the self was composed of three different components: self-image, self-esteem or self-worth, and the ideal self. These three components are important to consider when attempting to answer the question "Who am I?" What is your image of yourself as defined above? How much do you value your life? Do you value what you offer to the world? What is your vision of your ideal self?

Rogers believed Maslow's hierarchy of needs was correct minus one vital omission: the need for an open and loving environment. Rogers said that without an environment that provides openness, acceptance, and empathy, healthy relationships and personalities will be impaired. Rogers actually cultivated this mentality in his own counseling approach, which he referred to as "client-centered therapy"(in a way, this book attempts to embody the spirit of Rogers' idea by being "reader-focused"). Lastly, Rogers believed it was possible for all people to achieve their goals should these conditions be met. This will be important to consider later in the guidebook as we examine our relationships.

Following in the footsteps of Rogers, sociologist Manford H. Kuhn helped developed the Twenty Statements Test as a standardized way to measure one's self-concept or identity. Self-concept has been explained as the sum total of any being's knowledge of his or her self. In 1960, Kuhn published "Self-Attitudes by Age, Sex, and Professional Training," a study that used the Twenty Statement Test to research the self-concepts of a wide range of individuals. Kuhn asked people to answer the question "Who am I?" in twenty different ways. According to Kuhn's research, responses to this question can be narrowed down to five categories: social roles and classifications; ideological beliefs; interests; ambitions; and self-evaluations. The study found that the responses varied according to the age and sex of the participant.

These responses indicated that as individuals, we often answer the question "Who am I?" by referring to external aspects of ourselves. Sometimes people think of themselves in regard to their relationships with those around them or their profession, including mother, father, friend, journalist, teacher, etc. Other outward elements of their identities can include their education, their past actions, or perhaps, the amount of money they have or do not have. These are examples of external attributes of who we are, but they do not address the root of who we are as powerful beings, both physical and spiritual.

Other times, individuals answer the question by describing personality traits. They say they are caring, compassionate, hilarious, or impatient. But, again, these words are only describing aspects of the self, not the whole image.

Quite simply, you are not your job, you are not your relationship, you are not your physical or mental traits. You are something more, something beyond these categories yet composed of each of them. This does not mean it's wrong for you to answer these questions by describing your profession or your family or your finances. You should absolutely be honest when answering the question. If the first response to the question is to describe how wonderful your sense of style is, write it! However, it is important to recognize that these traits are only a small piece of who you are as a beautiful, free human full of potential. The more honest you are, the more you will learn about yourself — and the greater your opportunity for growth.

We ought to consider the possibility that the people we present to the world in our daily lives are not complete representations of our personalities. We might also consider the possibility that there are facets of our personalities we have censored from our own conscious minds. This chapter is about uncovering those hidden aspects of our character. Sociologist Erving Goffman believed that when an individual meets other people they attempt to control or guide the perception others develop of them by controlling or altering their setting, appearance, and manner. Goffman believed every one of us engages in practices to avoid being embarrassed or embarrassing others.

Goffman expanded upon his theories in his 1956 book entitled *The Presentation of Self in*

Everyday Life. He described social interaction as a theatrical performance where the performers (individuals) are on stage in front of the audience (the public). While on stage, individuals emphasize their best attributes. Behind the curtain, backstage, they prepare for their role. To perfect the role, individuals carefully select their dress and look. From this perspective, every one of us has a public persona and a more private, backstage self. There is nothing wrong or immoral about this. Each of us reserves the right to reveal ourselves at will. However, we can also take the time to become self-aware by understanding our true self, our motivations, aspirations, fears, and insecurities. To do so, we begin by attempting to understand who we are as individuals.

Look at your thoughts, your words, your choices, your actions, and your character. How do you feel about the person you present to the world? How about the person backstage? Are these two people closely aligned or is there a gap between the two personalities? When these two worlds are in tune, you are living your truth. The person you view yourself as on the inside reflects the person you share with the world. This does not mean we cannot keep certain aspects of our personality to ourselves or a select few people. However, once you are comfortable with who you are, both on stage and backstage, there will be less conflict within your heart and mind as you experience the freedom of being your true self.

Exercise: Take a few days to reflect on the person you share with the world and the person you are when no one else is around. Keep a log of your personal thoughts and experiences when you're alone, as well as a log of the conversations and experiences you have with the outside world. Reflect on the question *"Who Am I?"* What attributes and characteristics do you associate with yourself? Are these positive or negative?

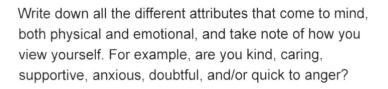

Write down all the different attributes that come to mind, both physical and emotional, and take note of how you view yourself. For example, are you kind, caring, supportive, anxious, doubtful, and/or quick to anger?

Consider the emotions and actions that you associate with your ideal self. Describe these qualities that you work to embody.

Think about your relationships. How do you treat other people? How does your behavior toward them make you feel?

This may take time to work through so be patient with yourself. Consider specifically the way you communicate with others. Think about times when people have told you how you make them feel. No matter what they shared — whether it's flattering toward you or not — take the time to honestly assess their perspective. Ask yourself how much truth there is in these words. Take time to note how it makes you feel to view yourself through others' eyes. Understanding how you view yourself is one of the most important exercises. Be honest and patient when attempting to answer these questions.

Principles

Question: What are my principles?

A principle is a law, doctrine, assumption, or concept that guides an individual's behavior. Sometimes people refer to this as a moral compass or a guide. A person who adheres to their principles is generally thought to have a strong sense of ethics. Of course, if the principles do not spring forth from an ethical foundation, the actions that follow will also not be ethical. From the moment we are born, adults begin filling our heads with ideas of what they believe is right and wrong. Generally, most children are told that actions like lying, stealing, and hitting violate morality. Whether or not the adults live up to their own standards is another conversation altogether, but these simple rules typically establish a foundation upon which children build their principles. As children we are often taught the "golden rule," the principle of treating others as we would like to be treated. This principle has been stated time and time again in nearly every religion, as well as in psychology, sociology, and economics. It is a simple concept – the notion that it is wrong/immoral/unethical to treat other people in ways you yourself would not appreciate.

Despite the prominence of this foundational principle, we live in a world where many people do, indeed, behave toward others in ways they would not want others behaving toward themselves. If the majority of the world has been exposed to this concept via religion, politics, culture, and economics, why is that we still see violence, aggression, and deception in the world? What causes individuals to treat others with a lack of respect and compassion?

I believe the problem lies, at least in part, with a lack of education. Children are sent to school to learn about math, history, science, and sometimes philosophy. But for the most part, children are not exposed to the concept of principled action. There are no tests or quizzes asking their young minds to reflect on what type of person they wish to be and the best ways to achieve these goals. Instead, the focus is on how to pump out as many graduates as possible who can regurgitate facts and follow their peers into the corporate workplace. Perhaps this is a vision of happiness for some, but definitely not for all.

How much different would our society be if children were encouraged to understand what a principle is and to develop their own set of moral guidelines? Moreover, how would our world look if we were each raised not only to know and understand our principles but also to stay true to them? Imagine the difference it would make if the celebrities and role models of our world were not movie or internet stars but people known for having a strong ethical foundation and moral compass. This is why our journey is pausing to reflect on the meaning of principles and to ask, "*What are my principles?*"

Personally, I have found the golden rule to be a great place to start establishing principles. We can do this by examining our actions and asking whether or not they align with this foundational guideline. Are you currently being dishonest with anyone in your life? Are you stealing from them? Are you treating anyone in a way you would not accept or appreciate?

If the answer to any of these questions is yes, write down those situations and the specific behaviors. Spend a few minutes explaining why you would not want to be treated in such a way. Also, take a few moments to put yourself in the other person's shoes and consider how they might feel after being mistreated. Finally, it is of vital importance to take note of how you treat yourself. Do you show compassion and respect towards yourself? Do your life choices reflect this compassion and respect?

In addition to the golden rule, I also adhere to the principle of self-ownership. This means I acknowledge that every human being is a free, beautiful, powerful, and capable person. I do not believe we need other people to tell us how to live, dress, think, eat, or love. I want the opportunity to live my life as I please, and I grant this same opportunity to every person I encounter. When taken in tandem with the golden rule, the principle of self-ownership guides us to allow each individual to live the life of their choosing as long as they are not violating the golden rule. If someone is living their own life as they see fit and not robbing, inflicting pain, or generally aggressing upon another free person (i.e., following the golden rule), then the principle of self-ownership compels me to leave them in peace. This is an example of my thought process as I reflect on my actions and the actions of others while keeping my principles in mind.

The final principle I want to share is sometimes known as the 7th Generation Principle. The sentiment can be found throughout indigenous cultures and teachings around the world but is most often associated with the Iroquois or Haudenosaunee people of the North American continent. The Constitution of the Iroquois Nations calls on tribal members to "consider the impact on the seventh generation" in every deliberation and action they take. The constitution, sometimes known as the Great Binding Law or the Great Law of Peace, states:

"In all of your deliberations in the Confederate Council, in your efforts at law making, in all your official acts, self-interest shall be cast into oblivion. Cast not over your shoulder behind you the warnings of the nephews and nieces should they chide you for any error or wrong you may do, but return to the way of the Great Law which is just and right. Look and listen for the welfare of the whole people and have always in view not only the past and present but also the coming generations, even those whose faces are yet beneath the surface of the ground – the unborn of the future Nation."

At the heart of it, this principle asks us to consider the impact of our thoughts, words, and actions on the Earth, people, and the world at large, as well as consider the ways our actions will affect the coming seven generations. When incorporating the 7th Generation Principle into your daily habits, this simple but profound concept can greatly alter the way you live your life and the choices you make.

As the principle becomes a habitual part of your thought process, you may end up altering your diet, your relationships, your goals, and your entire life as you consider the effects of every choice you make.

Exercise: Take a moment to reflect on the effect of living a life with these three principles as the guiding force. Write your thoughts in the space below.

How would your life be different if you followed the golden rule? In what ways are you not currently living in line with the golden rule?

What would happen if you recognized self-ownership for yourself and others? Do you believe that all people deserve the right to live their lives as they see fit so long as they are not harming anyone else?

How could your choices be different if you incorporated the Seventh Generation Principle into your life? Are there any choices you are currently making that do not take future generations into consideration? What are they and how can you change them?

believe these three principles could radically alter our world if every single living person adopted them in a sincere fashion. They have been extremely valuable to me in my personal growth and journey, which is why I share them with you. However, there may be other principles that matter to you. Take a moment to reflect on the definition of a principle and ask yourself what other ones guide you. Upon reflection, you may find you were subconsciously being guided by principles that do not align with your truth. The goal, then, is to become conscious of the principles we have inherited that guide us and develop an understanding of them. If they do not serve who we are as people (or who we are working to be), then it is likely time to reconsider and/or abandon them.

Take the time answer the questions in this chapter and use the space below to write down the principles that currently guide you and any changes you think you may need to make to start living the life of your dreams.

Goals

Question: What are my goals? How will I achieve them?

The aim of the first two chapters was to help you establish a foundational understanding of who you are as an individual and to understand the principles that guide your daily actions. As you spend time working and reworking those two steps, it will become easier for you to identify your goals and how you plan to achieve them. A goal is the desired result of an individual's efforts. This could be an object you want to possess or an experience you want to have. Every single day, each of us sets and accomplishes goals for ourselves. We may not consciously think of the goals we want to achieve or write down a list of them, but we are accomplishing tasks nonetheless. These can range from the mundane (running errands) to the extraordinary (accomplishing long-term goals through your own efforts such as saving to purchase a home) and include both the personal and the professional.

Whichever areas of your life you are focused on and whatever goals you may have, it is helpful to take the time to clearly identify what experiences you want to bring into your life. This means taking the time to be specific about your needs, aspirations, and dreams. Take the time to identify them and understand which parts of your life they pertain to. I have personally found it helpful to start by breaking down my life and goals into simple categories such as "home," "work/professional," "family," "health," etc.

You might want to get even more specific if you are a particularly ambitious person with many goals. Perhaps you have goals related to your professional job as well as your weekend hobby. You might have health goals related to both diet and exercise. The goal of this chapter is to be as specific as possible.

While breaking down your goals into categories, think of the big picture, and at the same time, think in the short-term. **How will your life unfold over the coming months and years? How can you concentrate on following through with your stated goals? How can your daily actions help you realize your long-term goals?** These are questions to consider as you examine your life and your purpose. Once the categories have been established, focus on how to achieve the goals over the next month, six months, one year, and if it's a long-term goal, five years. **Write down concrete steps you can take in the first month in order to get the ball rolling. For the six-month, one-year, and five-year points in time, envision where you want to be at those points and any steps you need to take in that timeframe.**

Here is an example of how you can make your goal chart:

Goal	1 Month	6 Months	1 year	5 years

I also find it extremely helpful to make daily to-do lists, which helps me stay fixated on what I want to accomplish on a daily basis. They also keep me mindful of my long-term goals. For example, when I make my daily to-do lists, I look at each category in my goals to see if it is possible for me to take at least one step forward. This guarantees that I am constantly progressing and not remaining static. This simple daily step can go a long way toward making dreams become realistic goals that are within reach.

Exercise: Use the space below to break down your goals into different categories. Once you have identified the areas of focus, create a goal chart and map out concrete steps you can take immediately and in the coming months and years.

Habits

Questions: What are my habits? Are they aligned with my principles and goals? Where am I inconsistent with my words and actions?

Now that you have an understanding of yourself, your guiding principles, and your goals, you can begin to examine your own daily behaviors and look for anything that does not align with your vision of our true self. With this chapter, you will begin to identify areas of inconsistency in our personal habits. A habit is a settled or regular tendency or practice, especially one that is hard to give up. Habits can be positive, and they can also lead to negative outcomes. Habits can come in the form of your vices (drug use/abuse, gambling, compulsive sexual behaviors), your diet, your work schedule, or your reactive emotional responses to various external stimuli. When a habit becomes ingrained into your subconscious, you will naturally perform the act without much thought. After a time, the practice seems so instinctual that it is often referred to as a person's second-nature.

If you have developed a second-nature that is made up of unhealthy personal, spiritual, and physical habits, it's likely you are unhealthy in your personal life, spirit, and physical body. This is because your life is the result of billions of small choices you make throughout your time on this planet. From the moment you wake up to the moment you close your eyes and drift into your dream world, you are constantly making choices that affect the direction of your life. The little things do, in fact, matter, and you can greatly alter your path by zeroing in on your daily habits and practices. By putting intentional thought into what you do from morning to night and asking yourself whether or not your habits are in line with who you want to be, you are taking a powerful step toward becoming the best version of yourself.

As you look at your habits, refer back to your principles. **Do your habits align with the golden rule or the principle of self-ownership? Do you think your regular practices will empower or endanger the coming seven generations? Are your habits in line with the other guiding principles in your life?**

Another important practice in the self-assessment process is comparing your goals with your habits. **Are your current habits compatible with your short-term and long-term goals?**

For example, let's say under your goals, you noted that you want to learn to speak a foreign language. You wrote down some practical steps you can take in the first month and planned out goals for the next year. It's possible that as you start to look at your habits, you might realize that although you really do want to learn a new language, you have not taken any concrete steps to do so. Instead, you see that your habits include spending free time (which could be used for learning a language) scrolling social media and sleeping. If these habits continue, it is clear you will not achieve your goal, or at least not as quickly as you might like to.

Let's take a look at a couple more examples. If your goal is to lose ten pounds before the summer but your habits involve eating pizza every day and a serious lack of physical activity, you are unlikely to achieve your goal.

Let's further imagine your goals involve emotional growth, perhaps changing a destructive emotional habit. Maybe you struggle with negative self-talk, and you wrote that you would like to see yourself free of limiting, doubting thoughts and language. You listed concrete goals for one month and six months. You are extremely successful at developing a more compassionate and loving dialogue with yourself over the first couple of months. However, after you pass the six-month mark, you no longer have regular goals and check-ins with yourself to ensure that you continue to treat yourself with love and respect. After a couple months pass, you completely forget about your original intentions. You realize you are back in the habit of communicating with yourself in an unhealthy manner. These unhealthy habits will find ways to reassert themselves (possibly as other unhealthy behaviors) until you take the time to identify the underlying issues that lead to these negative habits. We will explore this further in Chapter 7.

I don't mean to imply that you need to use to-do lists and goal charts for the rest of your life, but it's worth considering some method of identifying and organizing your hopes and aspirations. By writing out your principles, goals, and habits — pieces that make up the individual "you" — you are able to get it out of your busy mind and down on paper in front of you. This will allow you the opportunity to process each individual piece of information.

Exercise: The goal for this chapter is to spend a few days reflecting on your daily habits and rituals. Keep a log of what you do throughout each day. If you recognize an activity or behavior as essential to your daily well-being, write it down. In addition, take time to write down activities or behaviors that you recognize as out of alignment with your goals. Once again, you might like to separate your habits into different categories. Observe your habits in the workplace and at home. Maybe you want to study the habitual behaviors you engage in while around family. Think about the time you wake up, what you eat, where you shop, who you spend your time with, how you talk to yourself (your inner dialogue), and how you communicate with other people. Think of the principles you value. Are your habits in line with those ideals? Be honest with yourself when you answer whether or not these practices align with your principles and goals. In order to become the best version of ourselves, we must be willing to face our shadow — our darkest self — including unhealthy habits that we may have grown accustomed to. If you are not ready to directly examine your current flaws, you can always try reading this chapter again when you feel more ready.

The Holistic View

Question: How can I think holistically about my goals?

As we noted in the first chapter, the goal of the Holistic Self-Assessment is to help you identify inconsistencies between your thoughts, words, and actions. If Holism asks us to examine whole systems rather than the individual pieces, what does it mean for us to take a holistic view of our lives and goals? When applying the holistic perspective to our lives, a helpful goal can be to go from simply identifying the problems we see to understanding how our individual actions and habits are contributing to them. It is a fairly simple task to point fingers at external actions unfolding around us. A more rewarding perspective is gained by examining our own individual actions. By holding ourselves accountable and asking, " *How am I contributing to X?*" we can make strides in aligning our thoughts and words with our actions.

Applying the Holistic perspective also means we dig even deeper into our lives to see if we are living in line with our principles and goals. In the last chapter, we focused on identifying and altering habits that are not conducive to being the best version of yourself. Now, we will work on identifying inconsistencies in specific areas of our lives that relate to the world at large. For my own assessment, I have concentrated on three areas — economy, food/health, and relationships — but you may find you want to add other categories that relate to your personal development.

The first category I examine in my personal life is my economy, specifically how I make my money and where I spend it. In order to stay true to my principles and values, I have had to reconsider the types of businesses and individuals I support with my hard-earned money. I also don't want to support myself by making money in ways that are inconsistent with my belief in the golden rule, self-ownership, and the 7th Generation Principle. The same goes for food. For me, this category is about the type of food I eat, the source of that food, and the impact of my diet on my health and the health of the planet. Applying the Holistic perspective to our relationships means taking a deeper look at the quality and type of relationships we allow into our lives. The next chapter will look at our relationships specifically, but for now, take time to look at your life through a holistic lens.

Exercise: The last chapter examined personal habits in different areas of our lives. For this exercise, we are thinking about different areas of our lives that relate to the world at large. Start with your personal economy, food, and relationships. Think of other areas that are important to you and consider whether or not these parts of your life are consistent with your vision of your best self. For example, you might want to include business and determine whether or not the people you do business with and the type of business you engage in is in line with your principles. Write down your habits related to these categories and spend a few minutes on each, reflecting on any changes you can make to live more in line with your principles and goals. If you identify inconsistencies, write down an explanation of why you think the action or behavior is out of step with your principles. Spend time doing this for every area of your life until you are satisfied that you have identified all the unfavorable actions.

Relationships

Question:
Are my relationships in line with principles and goals?

We will now move to one of the most important aspects of the self-assessment. Each of the previous chapters has focused on self-image and individual principles, goals, and habits. This chapter is about looking to your relationships for unhealthy habits and tendencies that will not help you grow into the highest version of yourself. Think of your most immediate relationships with those you see on a daily basis. These could include your significant other, your family, or your co-workers. Think about other people you have relationships with but do not necessarily interact with on a regular basis. These could be associates you see in your social circle, at work or school, or people you interact with via the internet.

What is the nature of these relationships? Do you feel like your voice and presence are heard and acknowledged? Are you able to effectively communicate your needs within these relationships? When you think of these connections, what type of emotions come to mind?

Are these the types of people who encourage you, empower you, and elevate you in ways that help you move closer to realizing your dreams? Or are they the type of people who create doubt, fear, and insecurity? I am not implying that you should run from every uncomfortable experience you have involving other people, but you might want to consider whether a relationship is going to help you to reach your full potential so you can accomplish your goals. If you are spending your precious extra time, energy, money, and/or money on a relationship that directly contradicts your personal goals, it might be time to slow down and consider other possibilities.

I have mentioned that I believe many people fail to achieve their dreams because they set unrealistic goals based on aspirations that are not their own. This happens when we believe we will be happy once we attain the lifestyle we see in movies, television, and celebrity social media feeds or by trying to live up to family expectations. Our goals are often based on false realities and misrepresentations of a joyful life. We cannot rely on other people to define what happiness looks like in our own unique life.

Additionally, when it comes to relationships, I believe some of the biggest stumbling blocks on the road to fruitful connection relate to communication. Individuals often fail to identify and communicate their feelings and needs, or there is an abundance of miscommunication between parties. If we are not able to properly communicate and listen to others, we are not capable of communicating our need for relationships in line with our principles and values. Once communication breaks down, there is little

43

hope in expressing our desires for healthy relationships and habits. Quite simply, if we cannot effectively communicate with other people, we will have difficulty achieving our goals and working towards self-actualization, let alone developing relationships with these qualities.

Since, in general, we are not isolated individuals living off the grid in complete separation from society, we regularly interact with other human beings. We are interconnected and interdependent on each other no matter how much of an individual we may be. We do not need to give up our individuality to recognize this interdependence, but it is useful to understand the value of healthy dialogue with other people. By attempting to improve our communication and listening abilities, we are able to continue our own personal growth, as well as contribute to the growth of those around us.

One of the most effective tools for developing healthy communication and resolving conflicts is known as Nonviolent Communication. The technique was promoted by activist and psychologist Marshall Rosenberg. The premise of NVC is simple: Instead of arguing about who is right or wrong and who must win or lose, people should strive to have win-win interactions by focusing on ensuring that the needs of each person are met. The goal is to find solutions to problems by addressing the unmet needs of everyone in the equation. From a holistic perspective, the way we communicate with each other is equally important for making changes in our personal habits and principles. It is extremely difficult to have a rational discussion when both parties feel their concerns are not being heard. Such a battle of insecurities is not likely to lead to a better understanding of one another. Implementing NVC techniques can help individuals become mindful of their own hearts and minds and take time to empathize with those they disagree with. This lays the foundation for a healthy discussion and sense of acceptance among our peers.

The goal of these exercises is to reevaluate your current relationships in the context of your principles, goals, and desire to live in alignment with your highest truth. If what you truly value is to live the life of your dreams, you will probably want to surround yourself with people who also want the highest good for you, whether they understand your desires or not. Relationships and communication can be powerful motivators for accomplishing goals. They can also be a source of stagnation, doubt, and fear. It's up to each of us as free, powerful, beautiful beings to take responsibility for the relationships we allow into our lives.

Exercise: Take time to think about all of your relationships. What behaviors or character traits are you unwilling to accept from a relationship? In the space below, write down the name of every person in your immediate circle and those of importance whom you see less frequently. Describe each relationship. First, think about the practical details: How long you have known them? How did you meet? How are you connected to them?

Next, think about the type of communication that exists in these relationships. Does compassion play a role in your conversations? Do you feel like this person is open to listening to your needs and requests? Are you listening to other people's needs and requests? How do others respond when you attempt to communicate your own needs? Do they make an effort to hear your needs and requests?

Now begin to connect to yourself on an emotional level. How do you currently feel about this person? How have your feelings changed since you met them? If you have ever had any arguments or fallouts with this person, consider the details of the situation. When was the last time you thought of the incident? Was the situation resolved in a way that satisfied both of you? Are you still holding on to any emotional pain related to the situation?

Do you think this relationship is in line with your previously stated principles and goals? Why? Is it possible to continue this relationship while also living a life of principle and pursuing your goals? For example, if you feel strongly about the environment and work to drastically reduce the amount of waste you produce, will you be able to maintain an honest and loving relationship with an individual who does not care about reducing waste? What changes need to be made if the relationship is to continue? In our example, would it be possible for the two people involved to communicate in an open, honest, and respectful way to ensure they hear each other's needs and requests? The answers to these questions depend on the amount of time each individual has dedicated to speaking and listening wit compassion and respect.

Getting to the Root

Question: What is the root of my inconsistency and my fears?

Up to this point, we have spent our time examining our principles, goals, habits, and relationships in search of inconsistencies and destructive or limiting behaviors. The goal of this chapter is to begin the process of understanding the root causes of our fears, doubts, and insecurities, which often prevent us from reaching our fullest potential. Studying our principles and habits allows us to see where we can improve our daily lives while evaluating our relationships can help us identify and seek partnerships that will lead to more enjoyable human experience. However, if we do not pause to examine the deeper reasons we allow unhealthy behaviors and relationships into our lives, we risk treating the symptoms rather than getting at the root of our inconsistencies.

As mentioned in the last chapter, the quality of the relationships we maintain directly affects our ability to thrive as beautiful, powerful people. This is especially true for our relationships with our initial caregivers but also the relationships we establish as adults. The psychological model known as Attachment Theory describes the facets of both long-term and short-term relationships between human beings. Modern attachment theory was founded by psychologist John Bowlby and expanded upon by Mary Ainsworth. The theory posits that humans thrive when their bonds with other humans are strong. If we encourage loving, harmonious relationships, we are supporting the effort to create more secure and balanced adults. These efforts could see society restructure itself around principles and values that actually empower and uplift individuals through social healing.

Further, Attachment Theory addresses how we as individuals respond when we are hurt by or separated from our loved ones. As infants, if we are shown positive and motivational behavior by our caregivers, we become attached to them. We seek to be close to them because we believe we will be provided with emotional support and security. The theory was eventually applied to adult relationships in the 1980s when psychologists Cindy Hazan and Phillip Shaver noticed the similarities between adult interactions and those between children and caregivers. In the same way that children feel more secure around a caregiver with whom they have developed a bond, adults also desire to be close to their romantic partners and close friends. Adults feel a sense of comfort and joy when those they have formed attachments with are present. Reciprocally, you may feel anxious or lonely when your attachments are absent. These attachments allow each of us to handle the surprises, challenges, and occasional chaos life presents.

By examining our closest personal relationships — those with our parents, family, and loved ones — we provide ourselves the opportunity to identify and heal our deepest traumas. We can live our lives shifting blame for our actions to other people and external factors, but at the end of the day, it is on us to take responsibility for our emotions and actions.

Exercise: Refer back to your notes from our chapter on relationships. Look at the relationships you wrote down and any conflicts you may have noted. Especially note your relationships with your caregivers. Spend a few more minutes elaborating upon your earliest memories and feelings associated with these relationships. Remember to write in as much detail as possible.

The more open and honest you are, the more likely it is that you will be able to see past any facades or blockages your unconscious self may have created to protect you from deeper pain. It can be a scary thought to imagine facing your issues and trauma head-on.

This exercise should be seen as the first step in a long journey towards healing the roots of your negative self-talk, limitations, and insecurities. I encourage you to make an effort to explore the parts of your mind that might have been previously off limits to you. At your own pace, take time to begin uncovering and exploring any areas that are particularly painful or uncomfortable. The healing process can be intimidating, but on the other side, there is empowerment and growth.

A second exercise you can try involves remembering a time in your life when these relationships or attachment felt strained, damaged, or lacking a sense of security. Take a few moments to meditate on this event and really get in touch with the feelings you had at that time. When you are working through these often uncomfortable memories, it can be difficult to identify what exactly you were feeling. This is normal, and there is nothing wrong with having difficulties clearly identifying complex emotions that have not been previously explored.

Take yourself back to the situation and do not simply remember it, relive it. Experience it again as if it was happening for the first time and notice what you feel in your body and where you feel it. Take a few more minutes to figure out what you might have needed at the time. Once you have identified your need, see if you can give that to yourself in the present moment. For example, I spent several years chasing love and attention in various relationships throughout my teens and early twenties. It was not until I finally slowed down and recognized what I felt I had been lacking and what I was reaching for the whole time. I felt a lack of security and an anxious fear of abandonment. In this case, I would write that I felt

51

insecure, anxious, afraid, and alone. I would acknowledge that the emotions I felt were a direct response to my experience. I would also express my need to show myself compassion, love, and understanding. Remember, it is perfectly normal if you struggle to put your feelings into words. Allow yourself to write down whatever adjectives that come to mind — empty, lonely, bored, frustrated, scared, determined, etc.

Exercises for Healing

Question: What exercises/practices/rituals will help me release these fears and inconsistencies?

This assessment is meant to be worked through and then revisited as necessary. My advice is to regularly refer back to the first four chapters throughout your assessment. This will help keep the questions fresh in your mind and allow you to check in with yourself as you shed old habits. This chapter will provide a few exercises that may be beneficial for your healing process. Once again, the more honest and open you are to these simple strategies, the more likely you are to experience healing. I am going to share a few exercises for you to practice as you find them necessary. I suggest trying out each of them at least once and then focusing on the exercise that works best for you.

Journaling/ Self-reflection

The first and most simple of these exercises simply involves journaling. I mentioned before that I spent 18 months behind bars. I do not think I would have become the person I am today had I not spent the first six months (and many other days) of that experience writing down my thoughts and concerns. I started by taking an assessment of my current situation. *I am in prison and I am not going home for at least 11 months. Nobody can get me out of here, and I have no chance for escape.* Once I accepted my situation, I was able to begin asking myself: *How did I get here?* I spent a good amount of time working to answer that question and retracing my steps back to where I made a couple of wrong turns. I started to look at the root causes of my drug use and self-abuse. Every day I would write down my thoughts, wherever they went. Over time, I could clearly see how I made it to that point, and I also started to uncover some of the *why*. Interestingly, I also noticed my handwriting started to become clear and precise as my thought process started to slow down. As I became more mindful, my thoughts seemed sharper and clearer than ever. For this exercise, you will want to have a specific notebook for writing down your daily thoughts. Do not use this book for your daily to-do lists. Having a dedicated space to write will limit distractions, and every time you pick up this journal, your mind will know it's a safe space to be honest and real with yourself.

Meditation

As long as human beings have been conscious, they have come to nature for quiet contemplation and reflection. This is the essence of nearly all forms of meditation. Meditation is simply any act or practice that brings you to a place of contemplation or reflection. The consistent application of bringing one's attention to the present moment is key to any form of meditation. This means that nearly any experience can be meditative. A bike ride, a walk under the stars, writing poetry, or any practice that offers individual quiet time and presence within your own heart and mind can be considered a form of meditation.

Over time, various teachers organized their specific meditation practices into cohesive styles and philosophies, each with their own instructions and insights. These various schools of meditation taught different methods for remaining in the present moment, some involving the counting of breaths, contemplative thought, or repeating sacred words and sounds known as mantras.

There are also different types of meditation positions. Some schools practice sitting cross-legged ("lotus" or "half lotus"), walking, or lying down meditation. You also may have noticed that certain traditions feature symbolic hand gestures and positions during their meditations. These are known as mudras and are found in Hindu and Buddhist practices.

People choose to meditate for different reasons. Many people would say that meditation can be a religious or spiritual experience, while others find it to be a helpful relaxation and anger management tool. I would like to offer a few methods that I have found helpful for creating stillness in the mind. From this stillness comes clarity.

As you meditate, remember to write down your experiences and thoughts in your journal.

First, think of a time when you can meditate on a daily or weekly basis. The more consistent you are with meditation, the more mindful you will become in your everyday life. Once you have worked out your schedule, decide if you would like to try a sitting meditation or lying down. Finally, for those who say they cannot meditate, be patient! You can't expect to go from bombarding yourself with stimuli and distractions to a perfectly balanced state of mind overnight. Keep at it, and you will be able to start pushing past the static.

Clearing the Mind Meditation
In order to begin diving deep into your mind, it is helpful to start by decluttering your thoughts. Begin by sitting cross-legged with a straight, firm back. Position your shoulders above your hips and place your hands (palms facing up or down) open on top of your knees or anywhere else they feel comfortable. Either keep your eyes open and stare softly about four or five feet in front of you or close your eyes. Take slow, deep breaths, drawing your attention toward them. As you breathe deeply in through your nose, count "one." Exhale and repeat to yourself "one." Inhale and exhale while counting "two." Continue this process for as long as you can. You will likely find yourself lost in thought within a couple of numbers. This is perfectly normal and not a reason to be discouraged. Your mind wants to think, to fill the quiet, dull spaces with chatter. That's its job. When you realize you've stopped counting and started thinking about your dinner, your next blog post, or something stressful in your life, take a deep breath and start over. Think of these thoughts like passing clouds; acknowledge them, give thanks for them, and then return your attention to counting. In a five-minute session, you might not make it past five counts, but that's not the goal. You are not attempting to suffocate or ignore your thoughts, but simply to focus on being present and noticing when they dominate your consciousness. The goal is to simply "be" in that moment without stress or concern. However, if a situation or person

continues to appear in your meditations, it may be a sign that you need to find clarity around that relationship. *Finding Clarity Meditation*
For this meditation, the goal is to focus on one of the situations or relationships you wrote about in our earlier exercises. You can set yourself up exactly the same as you are when practicing clearing your mind. The difference here is that instead of clearing the mind, you will relax and think of a specific situation or person that needs your attention. Sit and take a deep breath as you focus. If you are looking for answers, take the time to imagine the ideal outcome and consider the situation from the perspective of everyone involved. Taking time for reflection during uncertain times helps one develop a predisposition for mindfulness over impulsiveness.

Expressing Gratitude Meditation
For this meditation, you will bring your awareness and attention to things you are grateful for. Find a quiet place to sit. Take a few deep breaths, breathing in through your nose and out through your mouth. With every breath think of one thing you are thankful for — an experience you have had, the food you have in your home, the people you choose to share your life with, your pets, the places you have visited, the planet itself and all the abundance available to our species, or anything else that brings you joy. For each thing you consider, silently say to yourself "I am grateful for…" As you take each breath and contemplate what you are thankful for, you might feel your body filling up with warmth and your heart opening. Take as much time to do this as you need, and when you are done, take another few moments to give thanks for

yourself. Specifically, show appreciation for your body and all that you are capable of doing because of your physical form. Take time to acknowledge each and every part of your physical being. Give thanks for the fact that you are alive. Take a moment to give thanks for this life itself and for your ability to constantly create the life that you choose.

Yoga

Although yoga is mostly known to Westerners for yogic postures, or asanas, the original intention was a system of healing that involved exploring deep states of mind to protect one from external distraction and transcend past the physical form through self-realization. Patañjali, the author of the yoga sutras, first recorded the sutras and principles as a guide for those seeking enlightenment and a path towards true liberation. Through meditative practice, physical movement, and control of breath, or prana (life force), one can work toward internal peace. Of course, yoga is not only about developing physical and spiritual awareness and empowerment.

The practice has been shown to be helpful for a wide variety of illnesses, including Post-traumatic Stress Disorder or PTSD. In a study entitled "Breathing-Based Meditation Decreases Posttraumatic Stress Disorder Symptoms in U.S. Military Veterans," University of Wisconsin-Madison researchers found that a practice known as Sudarshan Kriya Yoga can help those with PTSD better manage their symptoms. The idea is that intentional breathing affects the autonomic nervous system, so a consistent breathing practice, as found in

yoga, can help manage symptoms of PTSD such as hyperarousal. I highly recommend researching the wide variety of yoga schools available and developing a regular practice with the type(s) of yoga you would like to explore. Not every style of yoga requires physical exertion; practices like
restorative and yin yoga, for example, focus on relaxing the body and facilitating rest and deep healing. By integrating the asanas and yogic philosophy into your life, you can further develop a healthy state of mind and body. In addition, yoga can help you develop self-awareness and alleviate emotional stress that has become stored in your body, which will contribute to your understanding of the principle of self-ownership.

Healing Through Art

Art therapy is a form of creative expression that is sometimes used in the field of psychotherapy. The idea is that when individuals concentrate their energy and attention on drawing, painting, coloring, or otherwise being creative, they are able to express their emotions in a new way. The resulting creation is a representation of their mental and/or emotional states. The goal is not to create something perfect or necessarily appealing to others, but rather, to allow yourself to enjoy the journey towards creative self-expression.

Mandala Art Therapy
Mandala is the Sanskrit word for circle and is used as a spiritual and ritualistic symbol in Hindu and Buddhist traditions. Psychoanalyst Carl Jung is largely credited with

introducing the concept to the Western world. Jung believed creating mandalas was helpful in understanding a person's present inner situation. Jung himself also created circular mandala-like drawings every morning. "Only gradually did I discover what the mandala really is: ... the Self, the wholeness of the personality, which if all goes well is harmonious," Jung wrote in his book *Memories, Dreams, Reflections*.

Joan Kellogg is also notable for spending her life developing an effective art therapy model. Kellogg picked up where Jung left off by devoting much of her life to developing a system of understanding how individuals are able to express their deepest emotions through mandala art. Kellogg believed that individuals are attracted to certain shapes and designs found in mandalas based on their current spiritual, emotional, and physical conditions. Kellogg also created a deck of cards, each imprinted with different mandalas representing different character traits, relationships, aspirations, and the unconscious. Kellogg's work has been developed into an assessment known as the Mandala Assessment Research Instrument. In it, individuals are asked to select a card they like from the deck of mandala cards. They are also asked to select a color from a deck of colored cards. Finally, they are asked to draw that mandala with any color they choose. At the end of the assessment, the artist is asked to write down their interpretation of the experiences they felt in response to drawing the mandala.

I would like to invite you to draw your own mandala. If you are not artistically inclined, it can be overwhelming, so consider finding a mandala coloring book or finding a mandala on the internet that calls to you and printing it out. Write down the feelings and thoughts the mandala evokes.

Choose one color at a time to color the mandala, taking notes on why each color calls to you. For example, red or black might invoke feelings of heaviness or darkness. Perhaps this is something you want to express in your mandala. A shade of yellow might feel light and open to you and give you a sense of calm and empowerment. I always try to associate colors with nature — with something connected to the Earth — so when I feel drawn to a certain color I ask myself what the color relates to in nature, and I find a way to connect to it. Take your time connecting with the colors you choose and see what information you can gather. This practice is simply another form of meditation. It allows you to reflect on your current place in life and where your path is headed. It can also be a time to lose yourself in the creative process for a few moments and stop worrying about all the details of your daily life. When you finish drawing or coloring a mandala, write down how you feel. Is there a sense of accomplishment? Did any forgotten or suppressed emotions or situations come to mind? Remember, mandala art therapy is just as much about enjoying yourself as it is about reflection, so have fun being creative!

Vision Boards

A vision board is simply a piece of paper, poster board, or any other surface where you choose to write words, draw images, or glue pictures that represent your desired goals. It can also be used as a tool to meditate on what you would like to see in your life and to remind yourself of the steps you must take to achieve those goals. Hopefully, by this point, you have some idea of what your ideal life looks like. Use the vision board as a way to put your hopes, dreams, and ambitions into a physical form that you can look at and reflect on daily. By visualizing your dreams you can practice seeing, hearing, touching, smelling, and living the situations and experiences you are trying to manifest. This can also help you process any difficult problems you may be facing. Consider making a new vision board before or after major life changes or on a monthly basis.

Positive Affirmations

Once you are comfortable with visualizing your path and have begun diving deeper into the roots of your personal trauma, it is important to affirm the path. This is where positive affirmation comes into play. Positive affirmations are a highly effective method of programming or reprogramming your mind. We face external programming every day through the corporate media, the government, and those we communicate with. One way or another, whether by our own doing or some external force, we are programmed. The mind is much like a computer that can be loaded with a variety of programs. Many of us buy into external programming that does not empower us as individuals, but rather, teaches us to doubt our potential and capabilities. We can free ourselves by taking steps to deprogram ourselves from this destructive thinking. With daily affirmations, we can create a positive, compassionate view of ourselves and of the world around us. By using affirming statements, such as "I am…," we allow our minds to let go of negative habits and begin to rewire the pathways our thoughts take.

It's important to remember that these affirmations are most valuable when used in combination with the exercises focused on getting to the root of your trauma. You may find that you are capable of repeating the affirmations and putting your whole being into speaking them into reality but that you struggle with implementing necessary changes to create the reality. The exercises in all the chapters are not meant to be done once and then forgotten. The assessment will have the most impact if each step is continuously worked and reworked as you dive deeper into your heart and mind.

See if the following affirmations on letting go and forgiveness resonate with you. Start by taking a deep inhale and exhale. As you repeat the words below out loud, make sure to take a moment to really take in the meaning of the words. What you put into this experience is what you will receive in return. With both of these affirmations, you might find it helpful to write down your thoughts first. Use a separate piece of paper from the rest of your assessment (you will be burning this one). After you have repeated the affirmation and anything else you feel the need to say, literally light your thoughts on fire. As the flames eat away the paper and turn your thoughts to ash, visualize any lingering pain or burden being lifted off your shoulders and disintegrating with the fire. All of that stress and heaviness is returning to the earth. Let it go and move forward.

Letting Go of the Past

This affirmation is oriented around letting go of unhealthy attachments and regrets. I hesitate to call our actions mistakes because there are always lessons to be gained from all situations.
However, we can still recognize the value of learning how our actions have consequences. These consequences affect not only us but other people, as well. While the next affirmation will focus more specifically on forgiveness, this one is about letting go. Take the time to acknowledge the past, learn the lessons, let go of the situation, and move forward in the healthiest way possible.

Today, in this moment, I choose to reflect on any and all situations that might not be contributing to my highest good.
I choose to examine the conflict, external and internal, and decide whether I can rectify the situation.
I choose to come from a place of love and compassion and make a decision I believe will be best for all involved.
If there is no healthy way to resolve the situation I choose to let it go.
I choose to see the positive and the lessons gained from the experience, then let go for my health and sanity.
I give thanks for these experiences and the lessons they have provided.

I choose to be in control of my life and my experiences.
I choose to remain open to new lessons and open to letting go when necessary.

Choosing Forgiveness

This affirmation is about forgiving yourself and others who you feel have wronged you. Once again, write down your thoughts, and at the end of the affirmation, set them on fire. Release the burden of anger and the desire to be forgiven. If there is a safe and consensual opportunity to share your forgiveness with the other parties involved, you may want to do so. If that opportunity is not available, then it is up to you to find peace with the situation, whether that means self-forgiveness or forgiving another person. It is important for us to remember to forgive and love ourselves. The sooner we heal and love ourselves, the sooner we can amplify that energy out into the world.

Today, in this moment, I am filled with gratitude for my path and the lessons presented to me.
I choose to see any and all hardships as temporary and as opportunities for growth. I acknowledge my past mistakes and flaws. (Say them aloud) I recognize these mistakes as opportunities for growth.
I ask for forgiveness from those I have wronged.
I forgive myself for my mistakes and flaws. (Say them aloud)

In this moment I am becoming better, stronger, and more compassionate.
I understand that life is a constant learning experience.

I acknowledge the ways I have been hurt by others' actions. (Say them aloud) I am healing from these actions and forgiving those who have put me through pain.
I see these bumps in the road as possibilities for better outcomes.
I remain committed to my path as a beautiful, free, independent human being. Today I choose (What do you want to manifest today?).

Action Plan

Question: What steps will I take to integrate these exercises and knowledge?

You have now completed the holistic self-assessment and worked through several exercises to help implement changes that are necessary for you to reach your goals. As previously mentioned, these steps and exercises should be reworked as often as you need. I suggest a minimum of ten days to work through the entire assessment for the first time. Once you have become familiar with the process and you begin to do the steps again, you will want to develop an action plan to ensure you consistently apply the lessons and the practices shared within this book.

To-do Lists

I want to re-emphasize the importance of to-do lists. The practice may seem silly, but I have personally found great value in being able to track my progress on a daily basis as I work toward larger goals. Remember to keep your long-term goals in mind when making daily to-do lists. Look back to the short-term and long-term goals you noted in Chapter 3 and make it your daily goal to take one step forward in as many areas of your life as possible. If you have a long-term goal to get a piece of land and grow your own food, for example, today you can add "research land prices," or "research permaculture" to your daily to-do lists. These small steps will help you continue to move in the direction of your goal. Do not be too hard on yourself if you do not get to all of your daily goals. Focus on the most pressing matters first and then do what you can. If you do not get to a goal, move it to the next day. The to-do lists provide not only simple ways to track your progress, but also offer visual reminders of the progress you are making when you mark items off of them. If you don't want to constantly be throwing away paper, I recommend getting a whiteboard/dry erase board or two. These simple steps can help you more effectively achieve your goals.

Goal Charts

While the to-do lists are helpful for day-to-day accomplishments, creating goal charts can help you stay focused on the short-term and long-term goals. In Chapter 2, you separated your goals into different categories spanning different parts of your life. You identified the categories and then mapped out steps to take in the next month, six months, and so on. It is important to refer to these charts on a weekly, if not daily, basis. Make an effort to use your to-do lists and goal charts together. The goal charts and the to-do lists are your daily mechanisms for accomplishing your long-term goals.

Nonviolent Communication

The value of nonviolent communication cannot be stressed enough. When we are able to effectively communicate our feelings, the needs that arise from our feelings, and the requests we have for others to meet our needs, we create a space for authenticity to thrive. When both parties needs are being met, vulnerability and honesty can flow, and through that, healing can take place. I highly recommend picking up a copy of Marshall Rosenberg's *Nonviolent*

Communication for an in-depth look at nonviolent communication strategies. For now, just know that when one member of a conversation feels their needs are not being met, there is a good chance there will be conflict. Understanding and recognizing opportunities to compassionately express your feelings, needs, and requests, as well as honor those of others, is a vital aspect of approaching your goals holistically.

Meditation

Every year there are new studies confirming the health (mental and physical) benefits of meditation, and certain cultures have known about its benefits to spiritual health for generations. The simple reality is that when you make time for introspection and quiet time with your own mind, you allow thoughts and opportunities for new growth to flow freely. Don't forget that meditation is not only applicable when you are at the spiritual retreat or yoga studio. You can find time for introspection every single day in some way. I find bike rides to a very meditative time for me where my thoughts flow and I am able to process certain feelings that I might not have even been aware of previously. Even if you are only able to take five minutes to yourself at the end your day to sit, relax, and allow your mind to settle and see what comes up, you are likely to see a noticeable difference in your stress levels, and over time, your ability to remain balanced during any chaos that may come your way.

Sharing with Family and Friends

Finally, it is important to mention that if you find this assessment to be valuable, it will probably be worthwhile to take an opportunity to talk to your close friends and family about the experience. Share what you are comfortable with in a way that will help those closest to you see you are interested in healing. Perhaps start by asking them if they have ever stopped to ask, "Who am I?" Maybe ask them what their principles are and what goals they have. Start a conversation with the intention of hearing where they are in their journey. If you feel it is relevant or will be helpful, let them know about the progress you have been making and offer to support them in their efforts. When we help others in their healing process, we are simultaneously healing and empowering ourselves. Together, each of us will help our species move forward into a new paradigm where basic principles like the golden rule and the 7th Generation Principle will be the norm.

Track Your Progress

A recurring theme in this assessment is that each of us is capable of helping ourselves evolve to the next stage of our lives. It is completely within reason to believe that if you focus all your mental, physical, and spiritual energy on achieving the goals and tasks you desire — if you put these objectives before anything else — you can accomplish what you seek. This is the power of personal responsibility and accountability. This means you are solely responsible for whether or not you are capable of living the life you want. This does not mean other people will not make things difficult or that life will not throw you curveballs. However, the way you respond to these situations and to other people's actions is what determines your character and your ability to pursue your dreams in the face of adversity.

Life will never completely conform to your needs, but you can learn to navigate these waters with as much balance and concentration as possible. You can have everything you want by identifying your inconsistent actions, examining the root of your trauma, and taking steps to heal. When individual healing is coupled with real-world action in line with your principles, it is inevitable that you will advance towards your goals. I have done my best to present thought experiments, exercises, and tips that have allowed me to pursue the life of my dreams. It is a continuous learning process, and I make no claims that this short guide can solve every issue.

If you have an idea for another exercise that works well for you, write it down below. Try to think of specific ways you can hold yourself accountable. Even though you are ultimately responsible for your actions, having a group to study and discuss the assessment with can help keep each other accountable. Use the final blank pages to work through your assessment on a regular basis.

Thank you for taking the time for introspection, reflection, and taking tangible steps towards healing yourself and others.

Made in United States
North Haven, CT
15 July 2023

39051203R00046